PRAISE FOR *Hunger S*

FROM PROFESSIONALS IN RECOVERY WORK

"Carolyn Jennings has written a collection of poems that plumb the depths of an eating disorder experience. In a rich metaphorical exploration of that experience she tells us of her pain and of her emergence from the exile of her eating disorder redolent of the existential work of Albert Camus. Carolyn's journey in verse takes us along in the recovery process and describes her ultimate freedom from the prison of her disorder. Other sufferers will surely resonate with her verbal images. I heartily recommend *Hunger Speaks* to any lover of poetic expression, eating disordered or not."

Emmett R. Bishop Jr., MD, FAED, CEDS
Medical Director of the Eating Recovery Center,
Past President of the International Association of
Eating Disorder Professionals

"*Hunger Speaks* to the raw pain as well as to the resilient spirit within us. I am moved and inspired by Carolyn Jennings' deft use of poetry to explore the layers of story that emerge from her experience. The therapeutic writing community will celebrate a fresh new model for diving deep and surfacing strengthened and empowered."

Kathleen Adams, LPC
Director of the Center for Journal Therapy,
Author of *Journal to the Self*

"Carolyn Jennings' memoir, *Hunger Speaks*, is a poetic portrayal of a woman's triumph through the tenacious grip of an eating disorder and into the celebratory arms of recovery and renewal. The story is told through well-crafted poems that address slivers of awareness, passing perceptions and permanent fixtures of both peace and possibility.

The book begins with the section called "Sugared Hush" and emphasizes the feelings of being choked into silence by "all hunger and no self." During the realization phase, the author offers the section, "Bones of Silence," where she faces unfamiliar territory and speaks of taboos and trauma and begins to see the outline of self starting to emerge.

The third section, "Whisper in the Belly," is where she finds what truly feeds her and sustains her in body as well as mind. She finally becomes a true companion and champion of her own spirit. She begins to hear a newer version of her life as other previously silent parts begin to speak.

The final section, "Speaking Flesh and Stone," is a celebration of fresh perspectives, possibilities and a courageous confrontation of all that lies ahead. Finally, the "habit of shame once set in cement" is shattered into fragments that can no longer harm or charm. Self renewal and celebration of hard recovery work becomes the new foundation and fuel.

This is a book of reflection and reconnection that will encourage readers to find the strength within to explore the hidden, shamed or forgotten aspects of self. Ultimately, it is a book that celebrates the accomplishments of hard work and appreciates the gifts of gratitude and grace."

Deborah Eve Grayson, LMHC, PTR, MM/S
Adjunct Professor and Author,
Former Creative Arts Specialist for The Renfrew Center,
residential treatment facility for eating disordered women,
in Coconut Creek, Florida

"Carolyn Jennings' *Hunger Speaks* is rich with images that settle into the cells of 'knowing,' the 'knowing' held in the belly of an eating disorder. Through phrase and feeling, she gracefully chronicles the 'secret language' of an eating disorder to unlock the treasures of its truths. She speaks for many as she exposes the emptiness behind the hunger. Her work is both moving and stark simultaneously, an inspiring and provocative guide toward full-bodied living. You won't be disappointed as you let the song and rhythm of her verse cradle and grow your own understandings as she leaves the arms of the eating disorder to move into the arms of her self. This is definitely a read and a re-read as the layers of meaning penetrate in powerful, yet subtle, reverberation."

Jackie Bay, RN, LPC
Eating Disorder Therapist for over 25 years

FROM READERS IN RECOVERY

"Imbued with the light of transcendence, Carolyn's exquisitely crafted words delight like Venetian glass, capturing moments and transforming pain into truth. Each poem is a sacred gift that finds my hungry places and fills them. By writing her own self into existence, Carolyn has created a safe mirror for any woman's struggling self to emerge whole with the right to own her own life.

Carolyn's words tell my own journey through a harsh and frozen landscape out into the dawn of forgiveness and a reclaimed life."

R.R.

"*Hunger Speaks* is a gripping story of one woman's journey from confusion to joy, the story of a life stolen by an eating disorder and then given back with the tenderness of a butterfly. This collection of poems is so vivid and accessible that you'll want to take it to bed with you. It's an invitation to befriend our own inner poets."

D.H.

"Beginning with a hunger in the dark as I watch my lover sleeping, far off in a world where I have no voice, these stories took my hand and led me through the labyrinth of food and misguided love, of unspoken sorrow and forbidden words, to a place where borders begin to shimmer and 'problems dissolve like chalk drawings.' In that place, where the yellow tongues of irises beside

a pond finally fill the grasping in the belly, I think, ah,
so this is what recovery feels like, and this is how I might
get there."

    D. Z.

"This poetry memoir left me breathless and moved beyond
words. It is heartbreakingly honest, exquisitely expressed,
and it gives me more hope than perhaps anything I've
encountered. The depth of soul-searching and recovery
expressed in the pages is more than amazing. The images
drawn will never leave me. I have earmarked many to
re-read. It was like a fabulous novel that could be made
into a movie.

    This book is absolutely a must-read for anyone
seeking recovery from an eating disorder of any kind.
I could relate completely to the poems."

    J. B.

"I am not a poetry reader. I don't usually gravitate to poetry
because I think it might be obscure, and I don't want to
even try. Not so with this collection of amazing poems.
The subject matter intrigued and attracted me, then I got
drawn in, way in. These poems grab me; their messages
are honest, intense, insistent, and subtle. They are
potent, strong medicine that has stirred up emotions and
memories and images from my past and my path. They are
words I want to return to again and again. *Hunger Speaks*
feels like a living entity. It really has a pulse. These poems
of healing will be rich and helpful to anyone open to the
recovery path."

    L. C.

"In *Hunger Speaks*, Carolyn Jennings shows us how, using the tools of writing, meditation, awareness practice and talk therapy, a recovery from eating disorder can be shaped from the same raw materials that gave rise to it. By sparing us nothing of what she endured and finding the precise words for that endurance, Jennings proves the adage that the way out is through. As a kind of promise, these poems demonstrate the gifts of integrity and voice, compassion and magnanimity that await those of us who choose to follow where she leads."

    K. M.

hunger speaks

a memoir told in poetry

CAROLYN JENNINGS

Roberts & Ross Publishing
COLORADO • FLORIDA • USA

HUNGER SPEAKS
a memoir told in poetry

A Celebration of Recovery from an Eating Disorder

Carolyn Jennings

ISBN: 978-0-9822015-1-0 (paperback)
First Edition

Library of Congress Control Number: 2009943561

PUBLISHER	Roberts & Ross Publishing ENGLEWOOD, CO (303) 762-1469 SANTA ROSA BEACH, FL (850) 622-5772 RobertsRossPublishing.com
BOOK DESIGNER & PRODUCER	COVERS & INTERIOR Sheila J. Hentges
ILLUSTRATOR	COVER ILLUSTRATIONS Original watercolors by Rosanne Sterne. ©2009 Rosanne Sterne. All Rights Reserved.

PERMISSIONS

Fox, John. "When Someone Deeply Listens to You," from *Finding What You
        Didn't Lose: Expressing Your Truth and Creativity Through Poem-Making.*
        New York, NY: Jeremy P. Tarcher/Putman, 1995.
        http://www.poeticmedicine.org.

CITATIONS

Norris, Kathleen. *The Cloister Walk.* New York, NY: Riverhead Books, 1996.
Nietzsche, Friedrich. *Thus Spoke Zarathustra.* New York, NY:
        Viking Penguin, Inc., (1954) 1982.

ACKNOWLEDGMENTS

Grateful acknowledgment is made to the editors of the following publications in
which these poems, or earlier versions of them, appeared:
        Bellowing Ark: "Sailing" (under the title "Sailboat")
        Journal of Poetry Therapy: "Apology, Belated" and "Frog Song"
        Wazee: "Garden of Silence"

For Terry, whose tenderness
holds steady against my hunger

and

In loving memory of Joseph and Leona:
what was once broken has been restored

When someone deeply listens to you,
your bare feet are on the earth
and a beloved land that seemed distant
is now at home within you.

John Fox, CPT

CONTENTS

WHISPER IN THE BELLY

SPEAKING FLESH AND STONE

MY INVITATION TO YOU

Hunger Speaks is the story told in poetry of a life launching from the ashes of disease into the fireworks of recovery. It begins with these lines:

> *Barely twenty and cresting*
> *with nascent skills, I stand at the helm*
> *alone, winging forty feet of sailboat*
> *along the gusts off San Francisco.*
> (from "Sailing" pg. 17)

This poem tells of a wild ride one afternoon shortly after I'd learned to sail. It holds for me an image of strength and a memory of beauty. This moment of newly found skill sparkles on the water all the brighter against a background of secrecy, anxiety, depression, and binges— all kept locked shut. Just out of my teens, I was sinking into an eating disorder.

Yet my tale of hunger starts not in the depths of despair but at the helm of a boat. That Saturday escapade full of hope and triumph sets sail into a story that ends in similar vitality but with a strength of recovery and beauty of spirit—a kind of confidence and trust that I could not have imagined when I was that young woman at the helm.

The poems of *Hunger Speaks* tell the secrets and stories silenced by eating compulsions. The poems are a series of doors opened, first to reveal a past hidden and repressed and then to move into a life beyond craving.

In the spirals of understanding that build the healing process, here are my often-stumbling steps from shame to esteem, from isolation to intimacy, from body-disgust to body-embrace, and from hiding in food to dealing with feelings. Running deep below each breakthrough is a path from wounds and scars through forgiveness and into peace.

Why tell it in poems?

In the eating disorder clinic where I began therapy, I was encouraged to journal. Writing became an irreplaceable tool. I played with poems in my journal pages and then started to read contemporary poetry, devouring words of poets who authentically expressed their particular pains and pleasures. Their work reached some part of me that had never been touched.

These poets gave me necessary permission, empowering me to peek at what had slipped under my skin unnoticed. Somehow I had been blind for decades to vast emotional depths swirling within me. What had been buried under my warped surfaces had accumulated—abandoned and festering. Writing extracted it from inside me, releasing it out onto the page where I could work with it.

The series of "Tell Me More" poems explore how writing and speaking can be a pair of keys to unlock the mysteries of pain and healing.

> *I learn*
> *I need.*

I arrive
at listening to myself.
(from "Tell Me More, II" pg. 58)

Hunger speaks in many tongues and codes. The powerful specificity of poetry unveils much of what happened in my early years and explains much that occurs through recovery. The poems of *Hunger Speaks* are revelations that break the silence of food addiction: moments that create a large gray sea flowing between disorder and recovery, between binge and restraint, between silence and speaking.

These collected poems cohered into the companion and guide I longed for in the shock and turbulence of disease and early recovery. The poems voice the pain and record the way out. This is not a prescription but a possibility. This is not a road map but a revelation of what the ocean of recovery can be. This is not a how-to but a me-too.

What follows is not the story of my family, though selected facets and particular moments of family members inhabit many of the poems. Each poem is a slice of memory, a passing perception slanted through my eyes—much like what you might bring to a therapist, a support group, or a blank page.

I invite you to step aboard with me and to sail through this ocean of discovery, putting yourself at the helm because the only thing that is important in my story is finding your recovery.

In the final stanza of the first poem, "Sailing," I write:

> *I lift this moment,*
> *hold it to the light, turn it in my hands*
> *as if it were a ship built inside a bottle*
> *held upright by delicate filaments . . .*
> (from "Sailing" pg. 17)

As you read these poems, turn the moments of your life in your hands. Poetry provides space for your own vital story. Let poetry immerse you in emotion through its sound and imagery. (You don't have to actively do anything. Just let poetry do its job as you read.)

So jot in the margin. Circle an image that stirs something in you. Allow your pen and your feelings to flow. See what my story reveals about your life and wounds, your loneliness and relationships, the dysfunction of your disease and the freedom of your recovery.

A memoir, *Hunger Speaks* can be read like any story, front cover to back. At the same time, each poem is a story complete in itself. You can read in grand chunks or small nuggets. To help you choose what you need, let me introduce the four sections.

If you are adrift in the lost days of disease, you may find a companion in the first section, "Sugared Hush."

Deepening depression and unstoppable eating are my closest companions. The eating disorder disconnects me from my life and condemns me to a shallow politeness with others. The disease keeps secrets. I don't recognize my own

> *longing*
> *to be seen and greeted, hungering*
> *to open myself like a gift . . .*
>> (from "The Grace of the Gesture"
>> pg. 27)

The poems of "Sugared Hush" are fragments of a fragmented life, of choking silence and quiet oblivion—poems of

> *all hunger, no self.*
>> (from "Becoming No One" pg. 29)

If you feel abandoned in the rock-hard days of realizing damage done, I offer the second section, "Bones of Silence."

In exile from my life and homesick for something I had never known, intuition and desperation lead me to cross a new threshold into therapy, where I face

> *territory*
> *never before charted.*
>> (from "Crossing the Threshold" pg. 38)

I break trail to explore what led me to compulsive eating and what continues to feed it. Blinders drop off to reveal what had been so inexpressible it had been invisible.

"Bones of Silence" speaks traumas and taboos. In a voice defying fear, I shyly say what I see. Importantly I learn I can be heard. I arrive at wanting more. I start

> *to form*
> *an outline of*
> *a self.*
>
> (from "Tell Me More, III" pg. 78)

If you seek a partner for the tumultuous, roll-up-your-sleeves work of discovering recovery, turn to the third section, "Whisper in the Belly."

The repetitive nature of compulsions allows awareness to blossom; when you recognize the approaching holes, you can avoid falling into them. Through conquering fresh footholds and practicing new routes as well as reflecting on inevitable backward slips, I write a map around the holes.

> *My feet traverse untraveled ground...*
>
> (from "Where Once There Was Lake" pg. 89)

Though the path toward elusive recovery remains steep and spiral throughout "Whisper in the Belly," I find what will feed me: diving into relationships, nurturing my body, befriending befuddling emotions, and sprouting a spiritual practice. I begin to listen to new voices outside the old stories.

Problems I thought were me
dissolve like chalk drawings.
(from "Filling with Emptiness"
pg. 84)

If celebration of the multi-layered strength and multi-faceted beauty of recovery would encourage you, flip to the last section, "Speaking Flesh and Stone."

My eating disorder no longer dominates. Fresh possibilities enter when I quit believing the damaging voices as they sing their siren songs. Anyone can learn not to follow the bad advice of cravings. Their

> *demands bruise me*
> *but cannot crack*
> *the encircling wall*
>
> *of my love.*
(from "Tantrum" pg. 117)

I nibble the tender flesh of replenished life. I let the stones of old stories roll around in my mouth, tumbling until they are polished into objects of beauty. Recovery brings many forms of reconciliation.

But recovery didn't restore me to a place that would otherwise have been mine without the disturbance and darkness. Recovery requires and hones conscious awareness, which enriches every element of life. Recovery is a quilt of affection and joy, of strength and peace, of kindness and release. Recovery partners with a spiritual practice and path.

I celebrate the ecstasy arising from connection of body, mind, and spirit. The poems of "Speaking Flesh and Stone" savor breakthroughs into a full-bodied life,

> *where the unexpected and exquisite*
> *arrive in small, subtle twists,*
> *brilliant and brief as wildflowers.*
>> (from "Hiking a Trail of Turns"
>> pg. 123)

I have found my voice. I speak gratitude. I sing praise.
When I stumble, I say my misstep out loud. My words join
others in a chorus of recovery. There are lonely oceans to
cross, but life beyond an eating disorder cannot be a solo
journey. We need each other. We help navigate. We follow.
We lead. We hold hands.

Hunger Speaks is my hand reaching out to hold yours in
the cradle of understanding. *Hunger Speaks* can be a friend
if anguish has you awake at two in the morning. *Hunger
Speaks* may be a story you know intimately.

Please consider each poem a voice alongside your own.
As my hunger tells the quiet disintegration of disease and
the diligent reconstruction of recovery, listen to yourself.
Let your hunger speak to you, and let your recovery break
you open to beauty, strength, and peace.

Sailing

Barely twenty and cresting
with nascent skills, I stand at the helm
alone, winging forty feet of sailboat
along the gusts off San Francisco.
My senses seize the wind dial and any ripples
in main or jib, scan under billowing white
my Saturday neighbors—boats tack and jibe
off starboard and port. Feet planted
on both sides of the cockpit, I press against
the bounding heel, wrap firm fingers
around the wheel.

Other hands coiled lines and raised the mainsail.
Wind-born chill has herded my older brother and sister
below deck. Yet only their companionship
could coax me under the Golden Gate
into the Pacific. Holding steady,
we navigated through ocean winds
even when waves slapped over the bow.

Now back in the bay, city beauty rests
off starboard. Solitary I lift this moment,
hold it to the light, turn it in my hands
as if it were a ship built inside a bottle
held upright by delicate filaments:
Coit Tower and all the white buildings on all the pastel hills
topped by silhouettes of skyscrapers like blank
pages, books about to fall
open, sections erased by mist—a draft
not yet complete.

SUGARED HUSH

Voices in Night Air, I

High-pitched voices from playground up the hill
screech and scream and scatter.

Lone sax wails
from the mall below.

Some longing within caterwauls
for something out there

in the raw air
of season's first hot night.

I shun car, shuck purse,
strike out on foot,

soothed by the sliver of moon
and sucking in sweet breath of lilacs.

How old was I
when any neighbor's car

led us to dash and duck,
hide from headlights

just because
we were kids

at night outdoors,
adults tucked safely inside?

We gloated barefoot
in grass smoothly cool,

and after cars departed,
sweeping away their cones of light,

we huddled together
to gossip and giggle, tease and tell

about what—I can not
remember.

Marriage Rhythm

Each bedtime
you flop naked next to me
and wrap your arms around me
until I am snuggled in the tortilla of you

just a few minutes
before you roll away
leaving my flesh to cool.

In the dark, the rhythm of your breathing
cradles me, exhalation
like the candle of your words
when you open to me, inhalation
like the long legs of silence
when you listen.

In the dark, your body curls
on its half of our bed,
your back toward me.
If I reach out with finger or toe,
touch your shoulder or leg, you
squirm, disturbed in your
slumber, your private
dreams, your personal night,
you pull farther away
toward the east, closer to dawn
when you rise again
to leave me craving
more of you, more of
something
I cannot yet receive.

The Only Daughter

My sister and I feed our mother
eyedroppers of water as if we are rescuing
a baby bird. Holding her hand, which no longer answers,
we take turns in the rocking chair beside her bed
through the night, nibbling sweet rolls
and sipping strong coffee
while our brother and his wife
fly toward us, and our father sleeps.
Her breaths evanesce, thin in final ripples.

Mom had left us long before. Before
the morphine. Before saying goodbye.
Without thanks or benediction.
She closed her eyes upon the last chance
to say *I love you,* words she never
could summon. I had watched her curl up
like a piece of crumpled paper.

After her death, I will sneak bouquets to her headstone.
Throughout her life, she had commanded,
Don't bring flowers to my grave.
Give them to me while I'm alive.

Decades earlier, my mother had brought no flowers
    to her mother.
She had not sat beside her during the coma of final breath.

The news of my grandmother's death came long distance.
The ringing phone fractured the morning
while I dressed for school. My parents' voices rumbled
from the kitchen, then Mom's bedroom door

shut to seal her with her sobs.
A mausoleum of silence followed.
I sat on my bed, not creaking a spring,
waiting like my shelved dolls
to be told what had happened
and what to do.

The required kiss to Nana's cheek in the casket
was my first touch of cool, powdery death.

In the cemetery, I saw a small plot,
its headstone holding our name
but an unheard-of first name
and the dates of a life
ended before the first birthday,

an early clue to how little I knew
this family I inhabit.

What I Don't Know

I know why I don't dial,
though the big red chair in which I sit
is safe in my home an entire city away
from his senior living apartment.
All I need to do
is press one button
on direct dial. I fear
he will make some demand.

No confirms me as the niggardly, neglectful daughter,
cold as Mom could be. *Yes* drops me
again as a leaf in his wind. The base of my throat
constricts, and the phone's lit screen goes dark
and blank in my palm. I know I can become that girl,

skinny in my All Souls School uniform,
planted at his feet, looking up at his trembling hands
rattling the opened Denver Post, a wide white wall
of small black words between us.

I say
to others that I only want to be seen
but—with him—I masquerade

as willing audience
in the dark, smile
on a shut mouth.

I am still the youngest child
who sequestered in my bedroom my tears and my brother
to coax my courage to enter the living room and ask

if I too could go on my brother's birthday trip
to Disneyland, alarm clock buzzing
every ten minutes, the signal my brother devised
for me to step out and speak up
to Dad.

Now age and illness have shrunken and stooped
him. He is smaller than I. I picture him in his tidy, dim
living room, seated on the beige loveseat,
the only sound, the neighbor's TV.

If I dial, I become a guppy,
opening my mouth to speak, only to close
again when his words won't give way.
If I speak, he is silent, then resumes
his one-way course, destination set.
Zen student, I know not to take it

personally. What I don't know
yet is how to step out
of this habit of shame
set in cement.

The Grace of the Gesture

Stopped at night at a red light,
I check—car doors are locked.
Homeless loll outside A-OK Liquor,
line the brick walls of back-to-back shelters.
A young Hispanic strides
across the intersection, jeans, dark
sweatshirt, sneakers spotless.
In greeting for the driver
in the car next to mine,
a grin bursts out, haloes

his face. His shoulders rotate,
hands rise,
palms up,
arms spread,
chest uplifted,
as if to present a gift,

his movement smooth
as daily prayer, natural
as Monsignor's raising
the chalice, warm as Christ
greeting an apostle,

sweeping me along like a cool
sip of dry chardonnay on the far
edge of a long summer day.

He reaches the sidewalk. His arms
dangle to his sides. The light changes.

I pull forward, belted behind
steel and glass, longing
to be seen and greeted, hungering
to open myself like a gift
to another, thirsting
for the thin water of my life
to be turned into wine.

Becoming No One

…inside the poem of their lives, I can't keep track of my own.
Kathleen Norris

Unexpected fog drapes the wall of windows.
All day I exchanged myself for a checklist. Now

a table of quiet white linen
offers unfilled wine glasses
skirted by two suede-dressed chairs
holding promise.

Over the menu, I serve this visitor, old family
friend, a question.

Vignettes and ordering,
chewing opinions and filet,
sipping stories and cabernet.
His mouth shoots his
monologues over our table,
one-way stream.
His

words blast down the center of me slamming doors shut
left and right. One long hallway of echoes.

His insistent need
leaves no me.

I could be the mute tumbler on the tabletop
offering a handful of pansies.

I fear he will see
I've somehow become
eat   drink   smile   gulp   numb,

all hunger, no self.

On cue
my best girlhood people-pleaser
performs my place at the table:

I arm myself in glistening
comments about him,
thick shield of questions,
laughter continuously flapping
like an injured bird.

I slide into the white-tiled women's room,
startle to meet my reflection in the mirror.

Look: eyes, bones, flesh,
fully formed lips
painted a shade of rhubarb,
stained by wine.

Secret

Gulp crackers, cookies, fistfuls from the cupboard,
curl into a cupboard, crave shelter.
Snap doors shut

on palms that push against my back,
prod me to be
someone else's good girl.

Cling to the yank of a different hand,
fist that pounds on the door, stuffs hushed mouth
with sweet sugared dough.

Across my face, this hand casts its shadow
cutting as shame
dark as a blindfold.

This hand hammers
the belly into a fist
handcuffed to chaos.

This hand cements
the learned choke of
cornered silence.

Can't see what anyone
could see: this hand
bears no flesh, only bones.

Voices in Night Air, II

The call of the sax on city night streets
seduces me under the stars

to probe air full of voices
but mum to my questions.

As its smaller version once did, my shadow
hopscotches under my feet, rings around me

to the sway of passing headlights.
At the college-town, cobblestone mall,

displays of mannequins teasing
in prostitute-chic behind spotless glass

and the liquor-pampered laughter
of overgrown boys in the bars

strike me as if a shadowy man
waits down an alley

with only his hot need calling
to a passing girl, nameless

to him, his hand
on his cock.

I stop,
shoe-captive and sidewalk-confined.

The tug of the sax
slackens. I turn

back, fidget
with car keys,

and remember yearning long ago
for this freedom now at my fingertips.

BONES OF
SILENCE

Exile

I smell of dirty sheets.
On concrete city streets,
people walk fast, just
legs, shoes, beat heels.
Something inside yearns for
breezes off fresh-
mown hay, a fragrance not
ever familiar, so how
do I know it, why do I
seek it? I know
only bus exhaust,
belch of fast
food, and rot of garbage
down narrow, shadowy alleys.

I push through revolving doors, rush
into books, search rows and stacks
of others' words. Until my childhood
speaks up, once smothered by
crisp pages hard covers stiff spines,
their right answer, not my voice.
Books only tell. Books can't
what? can't listen.

I itch for clarity, answer,
but didn't I say I long
for the scent of hay, horses, pastures,
where and what I do not know
what to question? Below

in the courtyard pond, golden
five-fingered leaves reach
up out of murky water. I discern

maybe a cry, a voice muffled,
shut in a back-corner bedroom
down a long, dark hall.

His battered Toyota
still running at the curb
outside the library, a man talks
on the pay phone, his grainy voice tired
and extravagantly gentle.

I swallow the sound,
huge gulps,

craving,
homesick
to call home
call what home?
to be called home
to know home.

Crossing the Threshold

Every place to sit is overstuffed, lush
as the ivory-colored carpet, every piece
of furniture set at an angle,
the bookshelves with spacious clearings
cradle small works of art maybe brought back
from abroad, even the tissue box
by the fresh flowers complements the decor,
the light subdued, windows framed
by sheer valences draped
as casually and elegantly as she sits

in chocolate-brown linen that could come right off
    a mannequin
in a sleek boutique near her chic townhouse office,
her dark hair thick in its pageboy, skin satin,
legs folded in a chair that could hold two of her—
tall and irrevocably slender, a reed, a praying mantis,
    a greyhound

—whether such beauty is careless luck
or rigorous discipline, I will never know,
our talk will not include her revelations;
she is just the type of woman I could envy
and despise—her wall of degrees and certificates too,
but she is welcoming me
in a steady voice that props
me up as I sink into these cushions
full of tears—

she is thin enough to step inside me
through the hollow in my throat
to probe the hole in my belly
for memories and loss,
to shine a light on fragmented maps
where fierce dragons guard territory
never before charted.

Breaking Trail

It begins with a nibble to the ears
of the chocolate bunny, harmless
little midday pleasure
or reward or break or
private celebration of some small something.

It ends with nothing
but a fistful of pastel foil.

And no one quite there
to taste
the ripped-off chunks in between.

But someone left here
with a queasy mind
and stomach, watching
what I can't explain:

this girl
who needs more,
this girl, quiet as a viper and as
quick, this girl who prickles just under my
skin, the girl, hollow,

who knows only two things:
comfort and then
the need

for more:
next, next, later, when? what? where? how soon?

Garden of Silence

The black and white TV brings Bobby
Kennedy's body into our kitchen
repainted by Dad to Mom's demands.
Orange flowers of wallpaper climb the dining
nook hugged by tropical-sunset orange trim
above the wrought-iron table where
Mom has set the portable television.
I pass through this flat garden, knowing Bobby

is a boy's name, but a man has been shot
and killed whose brother had been shot and killed.
I'd seen a bloody black cat in the middle
of Belleview Avenue. I had seen bodies
of other animals hit by cars, but this one
raised its head, looked at me. Later I would look

at pictures in a book in black and white
of men crowded in a kitchen, dark
suits, white shirts. One white shirt stained with darkness.
What is the smell of starched cotton, blood-soaked,
on a man's chest? Death, messy, wet, colorless.
Faraway in the Disneyland state. The bang of the gun

scared me when older boys shot the rabid
dog, my eyes closed, ears covered. This death
is a man's voice and a black train on TV, but
no clattering of wheels along the track
lined by throngs of sad-faced people, Boy Scouts
and firemen, black people and white, mute

on the screen in our sunny orange kitchen
where Mom watches in her green striped housedress,
Marlboro between her fingers.
I say, *I feel sorry for that family.*
But Rose, Ted, Jackie, Ethel are only names,
not people like my own sister, brother, father, mother—
only names like the rest of our family
across a country across which no one
visits. Mom sits, silent,

in one kitchen corner. I stand in another,
watching her, wanting something. For a moment,
flat images between us hold us.
I walk out the back door to my swing set. I soar

back and forth for hours, summoned after sunset,
reeled in from imaginings of faraway
places I could live—places rid
of all I don't know and can't ask—
imaginings of faraway people I could be—
secure in a hub of bright eyes following me.

Like a puppy in obedience class, I come
when they call, learn their rules, take my place.
At the dinner table, I watch
my family as if watching TV.

A Fan Unfolding

bisect

After the dreamless deep of drugs—
Daddy's voice ebbing and flowing
full of tales of Tigger, Piglet, and Pooh—

mysterious month-long tummy-ache gone
with the tumor. In its place is a slash,
flesh pressed together

by a braid of black stitches
from just above the unmapped unknown
between my legs to just above my belly button,

no thin ruler line, no pretty package ribbon,
no sharp marking of a road on a map
like the ones Daddy shows me on vacation,

this gash more like a row of churned up wormy garden earth,
red and blue and broad as a Band-Aid and thick
as if something had been buried underneath.

home

The morning after thirty days
in Swedish Hospital, Daddy
drives me to Progress Park.

On the emerald hills of summer,
we walk holding hands.

For dinner, Mom makes spaghetti
with Lawry's seasoning, my favorite.

exams

In Dr. Britain's office—
monthly, then yearly,
Mom voices her single concern
(*cancer* or *alive* or *survivor* or *blessing* never tumble
    from her mouth),
the surgery has made my belly grow too plump.

Puberty, Dr. B repeats.

Mom, whose slender teenage years
were devoted to swimming pools—
this woman whose wedding day
was expressed as *118 pounds*
(where was the wedding? who attended? how did she feel?)—
this body fed little during the day
(but nightly summer ice cream and winter bowls of chips)
still possessing long, slender legs in her 50s—

never finds her concern addressed.

bikinis

Summers of others'
first bikinis and midriffs
unfolds into
my time to hide.

Scar splits my landscape
like a road's center line
from fresh blacktop to dead end.

Report Card of Hunger, I

Morning's aroma, coffee with chicory,
brewed just after the alarm wails. Creamy
warmth draws me into my day, second cup
to my desk, but the hug of coffee

never lasts long enough. I dwell in the next
cup, the best cup—outside, busy, busy—
delay to avoid jitters, then dive in
—inside purr—to tend the afternoon pot

and heat milk as its partner. As a child,
I hid behind mother's pretty skirts until
kindergarten's first tear-streaked days.
Imprinted on siblings' path of straight A's,

indentured to any rule—school, church, science fair,
hide and seek, I hid behind teachers' smiles
and father's lectures on how high marks would thrust
me into college, his thwarted dream,

and a profession of respectable
income like hard-won his—chaining me,
class *whiz kid*, to jitters on nights before any quiz,
a secret only my mother knew.

Weighted, small I, to earn smart for Dad.
Weighted, small I, to please pretty for nuns.
Outside, I was parochial school's
red and gray plaid. I was a line of A's

marching down the right-hand side of report cards.
No was tolerated only to what they set before me
to eat. So at the dinner table, picky eater,
I pouted and protested. Hungry later, I demanded or sneaked

sweets. Coating the throat of childhood were bitter
ashes from the brilliant fireworks of Carolyn
exploding inside unseen,
secret, even from me.

Tell Me More, I

I want to hear more,
she says,
not less.

We wrangle appointments
into slots around
obstacles of two
calendars, and stretch
my checkbook's limits. She says,
I want to hear

more, not less.
The words of her invitation

hang in the air: strange
glittering droplets
in a winter fog, dazzling mobile
new to my eyes
and just beyond my grasp.

Her request forces my need over the steep dyke
built and maintained at great cost,
flooding me with longing
overflowing the weekly
45-minute buckets
of listening.

Best Friend

Janice and I swap all secrets, gossip, and jokes,
circle the lunchtime playground, two girl-planets,
whisper rumors of wet dreams and Playtex,
guess what cuss words might mean,
and giggle over what body parts could be called
and how they might be used in deeds adult and obscure
(a one-time, girls-only movie, actresses delivering menstruation
on a silver platter, was All Souls' only hint of sex ed),
but Janice and I never swap clothes
so I don't know why our moms
talk about our dress sizes
when I overhear my mom state:

Carolyn is larger than Janice.

Now colored to compare,
my new vision convinces
me I must be the fattest
girl in our class.

Never again weight and shape
unstudied as breath.
The beauty of best friends
becomes an enemy.

Confidantes, classmates, strangers
morph into a line of funhouse mirrors.

The Tease

Saturday morning is Frosted Flakes over *Looney Tunes*.
My older brother and I cling
to reruns as if our real-life, close-up view of adulthood
repels us backwards.

At commercial, we set empty bowls
in the kitchen sink. I reach for the bakery box
Dad has brought from Piggly Wiggly.
My skinny brother points at me, drawing an imaginary
straight line from my newly sprouted breasts
to my already bulky belly.

Your stomach sticks out, he teases, *more than your chest.*

I shrug. We dash
toward the Roadrunner, each grasping
a big, fat cinnamon roll.

Later the bathroom mirror watches me
stand sideways, running my hand in a straight line
from a nipple to where my palm is stopped
by the bulge of my belly.

I learn to form this line with my eyes.
After baths. After showers.
In sidelong glances passing shop windows
starring dubiously sleek mannequins,
impossibly proportioned.

It's perplexing: the words swirling under the fog
of wordlessness ask, How can this body
be so unlike Barbie and Skipper,
princesses in illustrated fairy tales,
teenagers in every fashion magazine,
Blondie and Brenda Starr in Sunday comics,
Laurie Partridge and Marcia Brady on TV,
Ali McGraw and every other star in a love story,
the pretty girls in bikinis at the pool
who smell of sweet perfumes,
who carry boys bewitched or crushed in their wakes?
How can it be so unlike the form
I, of course, knew I would have,
the figure of the Heroine?

This is the shape of the Ugly Stepsister.

Poverty of Dresses

Bridge games gossiping up entire afternoons
enthrall my mother. Cigarette smoke
cleanses like a sage smudge. Chatter escalates
into chant. Female hands trump demons.

Clean rooms enchant my mother,
her square feet of women's domain
where hope casts its spell:
life could obey her command.

Malls charm my mother, exquisitely
draped mannequins, elusive reduced prices.
Sales clerks and tearoom attendants ease
her needs with sleight of hand.

Luxurious clothes bewitch my mother:
textures, layers, tailoring and fit,
the ease of well-bred wool,
button-up blouses of cotton and silk,

no pullovers that muss teased hair,
no finicky linen, prone to wrinkle,
demanding care she can not give.
Security and serenity replace her skin

in dressing rooms. Obeying her whim,
styles and sizes swirl on and off.
In these intimate, curtained spaces,
she inculcates motherly advice,

Cover your flaws.
Never expose.
Keep quiet. Keep still.
Keep secret.

Pretty packaging whispers promise
until it lies in her Chevy Nova with the paint chipped,
credit card balances trailing
like the train of a wedding gown.

Home, she slips purchased pleasures into closets,
softest slide of fabric caressing fabric,
the way a woman might stroke
a lover's thigh or a baby's back.

Returning to a threadbare housedress, shapeless
as a vacuum bag, she targets tidying up after children
until each moves out into college and beyond,
alien domains, leaving her alone

with the husband she once chose to whisk her away
from a childhood smeared in coal dust, small town gossip,
and the poverty of dresses sewed by unwed aunts.
He escaped through feats of engineering,

she through the spell of dabs of Estée Lauder,
the simmering rustle of satin slip against nylons,
and the cheerful turquoise kachina brooch
fastened at her throat, the top button covered—just so.

Table Holding Morning Light

Floral linoleum rolls between heavy silver grates in the floor.
Sun of early day July floats through thin, hand-stitched curtains.
Spices of cayenne pepper and pan-fried potatoes

fill some kind of hunger before a bite taken
in Lucile's tiny Creole cafe clattering
with plates, platters, and chatter.

This could be A Grandmother's House
with its scuffed wooden porch and smell of biscuits:
a gray-haired and apron-clad crone would grin

as she shoos child from worn-thin, oven-hot baking sheet
with a gentle giggle, swish of a dishtowel, fine mist of flour
covering them both in voodoo dust

that could protect for a lifetime.
My father's mother spoke only Polish.
Madonna and Child icons stared down

in cold frames on high shelves.
Fear of her tongue and her frailty
made her a black-robed witch

the only time I was taken to her cramped house
before her death took her
to my grandfather, killed long before my birth.

My mother's mother's English
could not reach beyond her widow's stern eyes:
no biscuits, no baking, no side by side

nor hand in hand.
Her singular gift to me came from her attic:
an adult's rectangular, red, plastic purse

my cousin said I must take
else hurt Nana's feelings.
Such tender openings I couldn't believe

lived in my Nana, her house narrow and tall,
stairs steep, and furniture weighted
with dark fabric of stories untold.

This morning above my wobbly wooden table for one,
Lucile's open window draws in rose-scented air
soft as an old woman's lips,

redolent of nothing known,
except the something missing,
gaps my life has always hobbled around.

The hard walnut shell of hunger cracks
clean in two, the exposed meat soft,
the perfectly rounded half shells rest

like the chipped white coffee cups
the waitress keeps refilling,
cupped palms begging at the table.

Continuation

Biggest milestone to date:
my class launches from eighth grade.
Families dressed in Sunday best.
Mom helped select
my green floral midi—
hip, stylin', almost *outta sight.*

First time ever
parochial school students allowed to partner,
we sixty or so together since first grade,
an ever-changing topography, my map of this world
measured with playmates and pals.

Boys mumble with hands in pockets.
Girls nod with downcast eyes.
Foursomes of feet begin to stammer
across the cleared corner of cafeteria linoleum.
The numbers spill out
exactly one more girl than boy,
and I the odd one.

As if through a sheet of glass,
I watch on the edge
of that gray metal folding seat
in an otherwise empty line
of chairs against the outside wall,

watch the whirlpool of dancers and
the inescapable wall of parents
watching them, watching me

perch straight as a chalkboard,
mask mature, pleasant, calm
as this girlfriend or that one
catches my eye dancing by,
any tremble of lip hidden under my one trick,

a smile
pressed onto my face,
specimen mounted on a microscope slide.

Tell Me More, II

Over the wailing
of the flood of hunger,
I say, *I can do
a lot
on my own.*

She says, *that's been the problem.
You need
to do less
alone.*

I learn to say more
to her.

I leave our appointments choking
on all the more
I still want to say.

When I'm not with her, I hold
this pen. I learn
I need.

I arrive
at listening to myself.

Theft, Father

After school sun.
Backyard lawnmower hum.
Gray house frozen.
Bedroom door open.

His wallet—plump center,
worn and flattened edges.
I extract one of six
twenty dollar bills.

Dust motes in cracked-curtain rays
embrace my tremble, his loose change.
Footprints left crushed
in pale peach rug.

I repeat as thief.
He never speaks.
Did he keep it—
another of our secrets?

After-School Lessons, I

Dank smell of 3.2 Coors and tumultuous
competition of aftershaves,
the lights to my moth, lure
me from square-roomed days and textbook-covered
nights. As we prowl these caves
of new terrain shouting over Donna Summer,
my girlfriends bring the light.
Our laughter masks my hunger
to learn a new lesson:

something about me
will appeal to someone

under the din of music in some dim corner
or in the blurring midst of pulsing lights and sounds.

Yet here I sit at the table, surrounded
by a half-filled pitcher, plastic cups,
and purses left for me to watch,

audience for friends glimpsed through serpentine bodies
colored by the lights on the dance floor,
the center ring of this circus.

Worse, this young man from the next table
comes too late, swaying with beer, and not asking
but teasing, *it can't be that bad*,
when tears refuse to hide

despite my cultivated expertise
at sneaking them to restroom stalls,
Kleenex and Maybelline in purse or pocket,
slinking past eyes thick with mascara,
through clouds of hairspray, around mirrors
where they cluster: sequined
breasts, belted waists, and miniskirted legs
impossible to outfox

even in my hippest eye shadow,
funkiest chunky platforms, and slimmest jeans.

After-School Lessons, II

I perfect my performance as confidante
—requisite smile for any friend's excitement
over the new boy (when I rarely see her),
sympathetic nod for her pain over the ex-boy
(when mine is the calm ear to which she returns).
My friendship becomes a yo-yo on the fingers of my friends.
I watch. I listen. I lock
away the one in me who wants too,

longing stuffed in my throat
behind the steel grin.

Home is safe under excuses and lies,
pleasant with Pepsi and Hostess and popcorn
filling the big glass bowl, comforting
with teenage bikini beach party movies.

Alone in the light of the basement TV,
I am still watching bodies and loves and lives unobtainable,
but here it's entertaining,
even filling.

Report Card of Hunger, II

Duncan Hines cupcakes soothed through afternoons
at the kitchen table, schoolbooks as companions
in the hushed house, math quizzes to come.
Corner-store chocolate bars tugged me oh, so, sweetly

away from knowing enough, pleasing enough, never being
enough. Later came hormones, crushes on distant
seniors, and nights with girlfriends at The Pizza King,
then in *Seventeen* and gym locker rooms,

thighs, waistlines, complexions unlike my own.
I hid behind widening hips. Mother's diet
hints expanded the hole in my belly,
stress-cracks into fissures I fell. Later,

I became one student ID # among thousands,
companioned by nights of sleepless study, unnamed
demands with unseen fists, and the tiny dorm fridge
of an absentee roommate. I hid behind

running shoes unable to log enough miles.
Each dean's list and honor's award added height
to a platform shaking for collapse
with the next prof, paper, probe, all pushing up

toward a shiny career that held no inch
of me. One man saw—I believed—finally
loved me. I did not see to protect my self.
Alone among kind professionals, I aborted.

No grief allowed to befriend this *logical*
choice. Donut boxes gathered, stashed on closet
floor, mute as a tomb, among stylish shoes,
feet still striving to be pleasing and pretty.

Penumbra

cafe

I seek my friend's brown eyes
           gray eyes green eyes.

(Pick a friend, any friend,
           insert here.)

Her gaze darts to the tabletop between
us, coffee mug steadies her
hands. Her job her unemployment
           her marriage her divorce,
           her pregnancy her miscarriage—
her words avalanche.
I give the listening
I long to receive.

What can't be given remains
veiled. It splits me
from this table, this woman, this friend-
ship, her greedy real need.

We each pound
on the opposite side
of the same
closed door.

counselor

I wonder aloud about my friends
over a serene cup of herbal tea,
looking only at my own feet
at the far end of the long, green couch.
Words inquire,
            encourage over my shoulder.
Mirror, she reflects from her chair
what I can't yet see.
Calm hand on my shoulder, she.
She never touches my shoulder—touch not appropriate
here. Only words combine us,
            mostly my words—
seeking answers, baring greedy real needs
under this microscope where behaviors
that bruise and confuse are merely clues, clearly scars
in the cocoon of her eyes
in the doorway of her ears
in the space unfolded between us
clear as a table to be set—
            almost but not
                        quite.

She a blank slate, this obstruction
clearly my construction. I glimpse
how some intruder severs
us only when years
                    of safety here
erode
gaps to expose
                    inside my trembling belly
a puppy shaking with joy
          leaping toward
these arms to be held

and back against the wall
eyes wide, mouth shut,
          the girl.

friend

I have learned to hold
this woman's quiet hand
across the coffee shop table
under the coffee shop chatter.
Friends for years, we glide
into each other's stride, nestle each other's
unfinished sentences. She steadies my gaze with her warm
hazel eyes. Sometimes she calls me
> *dear Carolyn.*

Her affection cracks
> a crevice, ribs to pelvis,
releases the wagging puppy

and the shivering child. Touched,

the long, thin fingers of trust
shrink back fast,
eclipsed by something.

fathom

Alone at the coffee shop, I recall her
dear Carolyn, sun on a summer picnic.
       On cue
       a shadow enters.

I sip café au lait,
lips unsteady on the styrofoam brim,
throat barely open to take in.
I sit under the shadow
              looking back

until an unrecognized, thick, locked door   falls from its hinges.
What was buried alive returns to me.

I discern the phantom,
                    illuminate the body—
touching me as no father
should touch his daughter.

Shut

Scratchy couch. Chilly basement.
   Fall? Winter?

TV blaring. Mom worked every Tuesday night at The Denver Dry.
Dad picked up dinner at Frank The Pizza King.
   What was on TV?

Faded set of orange encyclopedias.
Hanging lamp of square, plastic tiles.
Blackboard holding his numbers guiding my math homework.
   How old was I? Seventh grade?

Low ceiling, white tiles. Deep brown paneling.
Indoor-outdoor carpet, orange floral.
Scraggly plants from Dad's office banned downstairs by Mom.
He had completed our basement himself.
   Was I wearing a sweater? Did I wear a bra then?

Night. Black. I am watching TV. Mom is gone. Dad comes down.
   Surely the curtains were drawn.

Dad is losing hair, growing soft, so much larger than I.
   Time to teach you...

On the gold plaid couch, scratchy wool, worn and soiled.
Fingers where I've never been touched. Wet
mouth. Tongue. Partially
undressed. He finds my
wetness exciting. I own no
body, no thought,
no sound.

TV's gone mute though
my gaze stays there
marching across the screen,
bright and obedient.

Through numbness dense as cement, emerges the right answer.
One word. *No.*

The stairs take me up. To my bedroom. Alone.
Shut door, shut tight.
                    Was my stereo turned on? Cranked up?

I tuck my shrunken self under
the pillow, the world on the bottom
of the pillowcase soft enough
to cloak everything.

By morning, mind had whisked the memory away, just a smudge
or two remained, a chalk drawing after the rain.

Loyalty of Silence

Tall as a runway model, I sit in fuchsia linen,
wondering if it will wrinkle, pondering shoes
and lipstick to complement it. Beside my polished
black pumps, the Ann Taylor shopping bag waits
like a loyal dog, the other dress he bought me
under frothy layers of spring pastel tissue paper.
It is before Easter. It is after Mom's death.
We exhaust our shallow bowl of conversation.
The waitress brings French onion soup.

from the beginning, you know.
The pewter salt and pepper shakers nestle together fetchingly.

She was what they call frigid. Soup congeals
in my throat and belly. *She was a peculiar one.*

Never.
I pretend
for both of us
the flush of my face
must be from hot broth,
though my father gives no notice.

I don't know what was wrong with her. She wouldn't talk about it.
Oh, I say.
It was no picnic living with that woman. I'm sure you can
appreciate that.
Yes, I do.

Dad says,
Your mother had sexual problems

She never wanted to have children.

Other gals were interested in me, you bet.

Oh.
The French bread is soft and warm.

I stayed loyal.
I work to swallow
my gulp of chilled chardonnay.

Well, good for you, I mumble through
numbness thick as heavy cream.
He says, *There were a lot of long, cold years*
between me and your mother.
Well, I'm sorry, my words say.
My tongue massages a fresh burn
on the roof of my mouth.

how things were. He picks up his spoon.

Crisp in her black and white uniform,
the carrot-top waitress flounces to our table to ask

Some of the secretaries.
One in particular.
Rhonda.

Mind you, I never did anything.

He says,
I just wanted you to know

how everything is.

Outside

Bars are never good ideas.
Yet next to the therapist's office
while I let rush hour gush past,

dozens of bars stand
sprinkled among lush little shops,
proffering quick fixes,
stools eager to float me
while I wait for calm within the well,

fetid water stirred and spilled in another session
uncovering this bottomless blackness bottled within
that swallows me with each step attempted through.

At this bar, I confine myself to black coffee and blank journal,
but something from the abyss sends feelers

up my throat and invites
the hum of a mouthful
of tannic wine, even the touch of the bowl of a glass
balanced by palm and fingers,
maybe a steely martini
where discomfort could curl,
small as the olive, roll itself to sleep
in crisp vodka.

I set down my pen,
breathe, wait,

watch
young brokers—trim waists and contoured biceps
flowing under fine, tailored fabric—guffaw
over a circle of steep, dark stouts, warlords
commemorating victories;

watch
women shoppers—tanned flesh
under white sandals and flashing bangles—
shimmer over amber wine,
conversation murmuring like water over stone;

watch
manicured couple—long fingers stroking
mosaic of olives in a stoneware bowl—
lean toward each other over gin and tonics
set gently between their bodies rippling
to nibble each other.

I sip these sleek happy hour devotees
while the steady throb of canned bass through speakers
insulates me from lives so lean,
shallow and smooth.

I slither over the granite bar, slide through
bottles at the bartender's elbow, slosh
into liquid the color of tiger-eye,
and puddle under the thick, black rubber
where the barkeep treads.

Tell Me More, III

Written words listen,
feed me back to me
one bite at a time,

begin to form
an outline of
a self.

I want to hear more of me too
and to believe I can be heard.

My sketchy outline and shy beliefs
land once a week in her lap
of listening. Her deep pool of attention
writes the next line.

Landfall occurs on a treacherous shore:
I discover I can be welcome,
wanted, worthy:
whole

only when no part of me must be shut
outside, muzzled like a bad dog.

I have three favorite words.
No, not *I love you*,

those who love
what they need
to have from me
drown me
in my silent complicity.

I long
to hear
Tell me
more.

WHISPER IN
THE BELLY

Apology, Belated

Confronted, you do not deny, defend, accuse
me of lying, board up into your traditional
wall of anger. Instead you say, *sorry,*

not a man understanding and owning a wrong
or a father salving a wound, but a child caught,
confessing quick guilt to dodge punishment.
You tell me you have wondered whether
that incident   incident
might   might have
upset   upset me.

So I learn that you held
concern about the intrusion
from which I had hidden for years
trampled under the stampede of my defenses as if
we had tacitly agreed to pretend you never touched me *there—*
     or there.
Your apology granted me by my courage to ask
leaves me again stunned and voiceless,
then curious about how
you witnessed my hobbled decades,
you who had undercut them.
Your passivity torches
my broken branches, long desiccated.

Finally clear as rainwater,
comprehension seeps in:

I at twelve had been more woman
than you were parent,
and that will never change. You and I
cling to that imbalance, the saddle holding us on this horse.

Filling with Emptiness

Steady purr of water pouring
off the waves of copper-colored tile,

gush of rain rolling
down the tall, steep roof

fill monastery stillness
surrounding my black cushion

facing blankness
of white wall

and busyness
of chattering mind.

In this escape from spoken word,
streams of inner voices tell all the old tales,

yet here in this cradle
of space and time,

new speakers replenish—
oak, frog, phoebe, neighboring

cow, monastery dog, every wall
thick with earth, and all pairs of hands,

palms pressed together,
held heart-center in passing.

Borders begin to shimmer,
transparent as mirage.

Problems I thought were me
dissolve like chalk drawings.

Craving deliquesces
into palmate puddles under my feet.

In the finally morning sun
on the final day, sparkling droplets

on the tips of the yellow tongues
of pond-side iris,

fill the hand grasping
in the middle of my belly.

Now the begging palm
once empty and emphatic

cups sweet peace.

After

I am driving down I-25, hitting 70,
running late. I am talking on my cell,
straining to hear. I am zipping

past endless billboards stuffing
sales pitches down my throat.
I am bobbing and weaving

through thick traffic, squeezed
thin. Who the hell was I
last week in monastery peace?

My hard-won inches of sanity scream.
My spirit strains at the seams.
My life no longer fits.

Welcome

A stowaway from the monastery
reveals herself. This foreigner
inside me plays nanny

to all the wounded girls
who inhabit my nooks and crannies.
In greeting, my heart stands

alert, a big black lab wagging its tail.
I do not know what she prefers
at meals, this clumsy grace.

Our conversations stutter
in a tongue I struggle to discern
and always sotto voce—

this awakened wisdom lost
under the rumbling traffic of days—
my constant questions

met with her silent,
benevolent smile. She opens
windows I forgot I had locked,

leads me across edges
of what once was dark.
Long-held habits disappear,

leave in their absence gaps
into which I tumble and spin,
search with hands outstretched,

finding these holes hold space
where aspen leaves chime in summer breeze
and nights soften with blankets

she knits from recycled yarns.
Mornings with her smell of ginger tea
and shadowless possibility.

Remembering her scent from a time
my head has long forgotten,
my heart curls up at her feet.

Where Once There Was Lake

My feet traverse untraveled ground
hidden under the waters of Lake Dillon
for all the prior years of my life.

Drought has so parched this land it barely receives
imprints of my soles. Dirt holds its pattern
of cracks, dry and hard, despite last night's rain,
gentle and steady.

Deeper into what once was manmade lake,
grass grows and flowers cluster.

Someone has built a lean-to where shoreline once was.
On family vacation, I skimmed this lake's satin waters,
my father piloting the speedboat, my brother and I snuggled
in heavy marshmallows of lifejackets, hair flying
through the sparkles of spray and the breath of mountain sun.

Afternoon thunderstorm whipped up
white-capped sea serpents.
Dad steered our bucking steed
to a sheltered cove, tucked us under cover.
In the blue cave of his crisp tarp rattling
over branches, I was soggy and shivering
on the warm, dry lap of my father.

His footprints of care, forgotten,
nonetheless left a path.

I Am

I lie on my back, look up at dull white
rec center ceiling, fluorescent lights.
I am full of lists and rush
and what I think and think and think
and should and should and am not.
One deep breath.

I close my eyes, heed the trainer's familiar
recitation, glide the Pilates carriage
back and forth, adjust, reposition,
raise feet, circle arms, partner with each
inhalation and exhalation.

I push up from the bar—legs stretch
as long as any NBA player's.

I exhale—squeeze navel to spine,
slender as a gazelle.

I row—back and shoulders
Herculean.

I lift my legs straight above my head—
I am Cirque du Soleil.

For one hour,
I am triceps and biceps,
sits bones and abs,
shoulder blades, sacrum,
twelve pairs of ribs.
I know each
of my twenty-four vertebrae.
Oxygen enters my lungs.
Carbon dioxide leaves.
I move only with air.

I remember
what will too soon
slip away again,

I too am
earth.

The Door to Hunger

An older couple waits at the only table set
for breakfast in the inn. My husband and I
introduce ourselves, and when I answer *poet*, they ask
how poems form on my page, inquire
more to my answers, more
about the process and how
I came to be.

Topics change. I remain
basking in their light.

                Over an hour passes over our table.
Even the white-cow cream pitcher pricks up her ears.

Packing after to check out and move on,
I rush
for no reason, trip
over things, snap
at anyone... but didn't gulp
coffee or pastry, don't do that
anymore... yet something's
pried my belly open

                like a whale's maw.

Craving forgets
the just-past feast, commands
all attention, a child

              tangled

in the net of a tantrum.

              Why do I still hunger?

Attentiveness
arrived over homemade marmalade
and stoneware platters of plenty.
One hour's worth.
Though I nibbled every crumb
of the treasure around the table,
                           I own no way to fill.

Eggshell

Home again, I find his Honda
still in the garage. As if limping around broken
glass, I step inside in silence. I unpack
groceries. Not quite able to
exhale, I wash dishes. My belly
clenches choked anger
inherited and unnamed
within the skin of my childhood.

Then, I learned only home alone
was a wide smooth beach, a calm
dawn sea, the absence of cringing
in case debris crashed from far shores.

Then, only home alone, my bedroom door open.

Today's intrusion shatters solitary
reign, rips thin tier of constructed
tranquility. The name *rage*
escapes me and, with it, its birthplace,
previously hunted down. Now
not even a search party sent.

My husband appears
in the doorway, face pale, eyes glassy.
Neither of us moves toward
a kiss. He murmurs,
he will heat himself soup from a can.
My gut shakes like a fist. His sweet body,
hunched in a bathrobe, draws

my breath to this kitchen: his sick day
is not the meteorite that created
this crater exposed in me.

We are both hungry.

From a room away, I toss an offer
of scrambled eggs. Before we eat
next to each other, before chat
breaks our eggshell of dead air, I crack
and whisk eggs, cut butter, rinse fresh berries
and spoon reds and blues into delicate glass bowls,
fill our home with Sunday breakfast lessons
learned long ago: nothing surpasses the hug
of the soft bubbling of melting butter,
greasy invitation of bacon, creamy softness of eggs in a pan.

Beggar at the Intersection of Winter and Spring

Beggar at the intersection sits curled under thin
sweatshirt hood, cardboard request shimmying in the gusts,
face hidden behind knees bared in frayed jeans,
   no hand held out,
just as my father would turn away
from watching my life to tell again stories of his.
My car window kept shut tight
   as I am with my father,
only imagining who I would be
if I could reach through my anger at his temper,
my hurt over how he could never see
   past his own empty hands
though his wife, his kids—we all gave ourselves
to try to fill them
and never ask of them,
   my bedroom door kept shut.
Dusk sky ushers rain tonight.
The heat in the closed car flushes my face.
An edge of light the color of ash
   hangs on the horizon.
Around the edges of night, outside
the gaze of my mother,
my father might reach out,
   pin my girl bones
between blond wood cupboards and the bulk
of his body needing anyone's attention.
This beggar appears more abandoned than abusive,
   but wasn't that also my father,

who couldn't conjure hands to steady his children
out of the hollow pockets of his childhood,
spirit as crushed as the dead sparrow in the gutter?
            When birds fly, connection
is essential in migration.
Yet my flight from family, internal, echoes
how my father settled us far from his birth,
            each attempting only to save ourselves.
I hunger now to unlock my doors of steel,
but, unsure the cost, I refuse
to let down glass walls,
            to extend a hand,
to empty my palms, letting what I think I've earned
into the wind, to be what I can
to one left out in blustery cold,
            this beggar, my father, my self.

Shifting Light of Darkness

Startling the stillness out of morning-walk woods,
forty or fifty birds carpet the meadow
between me and home
with dusk that breathes in and out.

Crows resettle themselves one by one,
avian chess match
under air gray and silver
ushering mist and chill.

Dark feathers flash above golden grass,
unveiling colors astride the black:
blue, green, purple
of jewels, gemstones, blown glass.

Finely muscled elegance
sings in sibilance
from wings ready for game, mischief, or revolution,
each toe and beak tipped by creativity.

Royalty of sharp eye and fierce cry spread for my view,
each becomes an inkwell of promise
for a pen that feathers darkness
into slants of light.

Rock, River, Shadow

I held my father's hand
when we would walk the river's edge
handpicking our bucketful of smooth stones,
aficionados of rocks.

Colorado late-day sun
on our silver bucket
mirrored water's dance
as if fireflies were finger painting.

Back in the basement alone,
he worked with paint and glue
firmly in their places before him.
He conjured animals and people out of rocks

to inhabit my bedroom bookcase,
his bits of felt and sparkly
glass were fur and diamonds
in my eyes, his *baby girl*.

Baby girl was the one outside All Souls Church
Sunday morning in my preschool years
who saw that my father walked in our gravitational pull
but left to his own orbit, shoulders stuck in their hunch.

I began to extend my hand to his.
Now his term of endearment *baby girl*
pokes like a pebble in my shoe.
If with him, my bones turn to stone.

Yet the glass and sequin eyes
of the rock menagerie still wink
from my bookshelves, twinkle like his blue eyes,
cut through all that lies between,

leaving me bereft
to explain even to myself
forces strong enough
to split rock.

Courtship

Listless, I am
weighted. I want
only to be a shield,
nothing
in, nothing out, vulnerability
tucked tight. Sadness casts
a long shadow.

Obligations call.
I wish I could erase
me, draw myself already at
today's destination, color
my blank spots in pastels.

I drive past a flock of black birds spiraling
slinky-like from one bush to another.

KBCO offers the B-52s, tempts
vocal chords back to college days:
shoulders could turn
suddenly sexy and sway.

Throat remains a stone.
But in the rock of body, hips
begin to grin.

Though sunglasses keep my gaze dark,
mountain peaks fresh
with last night's white
flaunt the Continental Divide
until its beauty dazzles me.

Face to face with my first human,
the brightness of eyes catch me,

blue islands amid wrinkles, this waitress' eyes.
She hands me a menu, pours a coffee, allows words

to pour from my mouth, pleasant and kind
rather than miserable and miserly.
When she fumbles the flatware,
our soft laughter
braids the surrounding air,
erases all else,

joins us
as girlfriends holding hands at recess.

How is it that the world insists
on rising to carry me over its threshold
despite all I do to let it pass, ditch it,
give it the cold shoulder?
We grieve each other,
this life and I, but it is Life who later appears
at my doorstep with a dozen roses
and a beguiling grin.

End of the Affair

Delay home alone. Husband
away, business. When I arrive, loneliness

howls a welcome.
On its heels marches an urge,

a little late night snack,
an offer to ease

my empty bed. Tonight I choose to indulge
hollowness only. Confronted,

sadness dashes,
leaving behind long, scaly shadows:

cravings linger, whisper, charm, seduce,
beg, jab, rage.

I refuse this con
whose promise rings hollow,

gone tomorrow. I resign myself to be an old maid
this time.

Lament amplifies
as I abandon my dear hero,

forbidden pleasure,
food as comfort.

Red Sweater

Yesterday's red sweater
hangs on the back of the dining chair
across from me at breakfast.

Yesterday it cradled my flesh
with body's own heat,
reflected me back to me.

Its heavy threads marked
my borders the way an animal
marks territory.

It showed the world its pattern
of cotton moons and stars, its bold
redness, as if telling something about me.

Yesterday's cocoon hangs empty.

Sometimes

Sometimes I step
out of depression,
stare back
at self hatred,
eye to eye.

Hatred quivers and fades.
Depression's hollow armor
clangs to the floor, echoes,
leaving me
naked and cold.

I stare at the hollows
from a near distance. Those intimate spots
plump up their pillows and exhort,
a forsaken lover primped to repossess
one who slipped away,
or from behind comes a tap on my shoulder
and a whisper like a best friend
or a mother.

Sometimes I decline the invitation to old comforts,
move forward,
                stumble onto
                        spring green grass underfoot.

Even as days and seasons
lurch and totter,
a thread of silkiness
like the scented touch

of a summer shower
on tender flesh
continues
        to beckon,
                nascent whisper,

the way another mother might
kneel, reassure, relish
a toddler's steps.

Alleluia (Leona's Story)

Eternal and formal in stone, her name.
I kiss my fingers, press them to the hollows
of the five letters, keep quiet close.

> *Never a mama of breast milk or home-*
> *baked bread, she was a mom of Campbell's soup*
> *casseroles, Taster's Choice, and Marlboros.*

Gray as Leona's hair, a storm
gathers silver sky. Gusts and small creatures
rattle leaves of cemetery trees,
spirits preparing for redemption.

> *She could never leave the steady provider,*
> *the husband she blamed again and again.*
> *She could not risk a return to—what?—*
> *the small town gossip she'd been eager*
> *to flee, poverty never spoken or*
> *was there something else—something left*
> *behind, indelible and ineffable?*

I hold her story, Leona's story,
words shot through my pen like a syringe
to mend pain. Bolts of lightning had split me
from others, illuminated how I wilt
because long ago wounds parched her
affection, constricted what could flow between
us. Her brittle sun withered my sweet seeds.

Anger sizzled and sadness swelled. For long,
random stretches, no floor scrubbed, no skirt ironed,
no gift bought could please. She started to say,
My wardrobe is better than my life.

I wrote her story, Leona's story,
to scribe her side of our seesaw of ache,
to sketch a map broader than my singular
pain—to guide me home.

More evenings she spent alone on her twin bed
playing solitaire, cards shuffled and flipped
in nightly silence, after bridge club disbanded,
after the marriage bed abandoned.

Above the grave, a Canada goose flaps,
handsome, dignified, and solitary
as the life Leona knit from frayed thread.
I read her story aloud. After the sounds spill
into wind, I sprinkle ashes, burned words,
on the ground by her headstone, gray powder
soothing as talcum. I become liquid
as the mute despair clouding Leona's eyes.

At age fifty, she tried to learn to ride
a bike that summer—mornings in Washington
Park by the peace of the lake, me zipping
on my little red Schwinn around her
wobbling on my sister's rusted brown bike.

Wet on stone and skin, first drops splash, soft
as ash. Arid land relinquishes old dust.

> *She sat primped and upright at every*
> *elementary school function. She gave*
> *me the prettiest holiday dresses,*
> *Easter cookies to ice and ducklings*
> *to cuddle, chocolate shakes after*
> *the dentist, front-row seats at Swan Lake*
> *and Nutcracker—treats her childhood lacked.*
> *Back then, she was Erma Bombeck*
> *read aloud over Bisquick waffles on Sunday*
> *mornings until laughter embraced us all.*

Open Palm of the Day

Before breakfast, I squeeze laundry overflowing
its baskets into open-mouthed machines. While
my hand brushes my teeth, my head races
the day's errands. Clutching briefcase and bag lunch,
my husband pecks my cheek, not an obligatory once
but a flirtatious twice.
The door closes on the tickling
sweet scent of his washed hair.
My hand caresses my face
alive where he planted his warmth.

Open afternoon window invites velvet air,
heavy under passing gray. Squabbles
of finches enter from the feeder and mingle
with the dribble of a basketball down the street.
Rajah, usually aristocratically distant,
curls into my lap, his furred body
making my legs purr
on this spring day turned raw.
Though my bulging notebook wobbles
and my bladder nudges me,
I preserve our stillness.

Worn at day's end, I lean against
our cluttered counter, sniff
chicken baking with rosemary, sip
sparkling water from a chipped glass,
tile smooth and cool under stubbornly bare feet.
Ashes of the past settle softly,
now mostly compost.

A square of western sun slides
onto my feet, a welcome
mat into this particular evening
that wins me for itself.
I am nowhere else.

SPEAKING FLESH
AND STONE

Alchemy

I would believe only in a god who could dance.
Friedrich Nietzsche

dance begins for me as mystery
watching other bodies
elongated ecstatic elegant elastic
a species foreign

I step around what feels like myself
to move in voodoo joy
dance sweeping up
all of me, no room left for uncertainty

open palm
      or tight fist, the hand of dance
shakes out   possibility
      foams colors   like baths of bubbles

I dance fuchsia acrylic on silk
      sage pastel on linen
            gold calligraphy stroking midnight

I dance in tongues I dance no words   between the lines I dance
      new strokes and nonsense rhymes
          body let off its leash
            leads
        nothing need make sense in dance
           and suddenly   everything does

god dwells in the body and dance is   the hymn of praise
the limbs of gospel the wings   of dharma

I dance only for the god who believes only in me

I dance through air
        thin
                as rain
                        or thick
                                as grit
                                        I dance Grand

                        Marnier on sharpwinternight and black
                        coffee at pinkdaybreak and tart
                        limeade on summerhotsand

                I dance flags of every country flapping
                                on parade
                                under blue
                        I dance tribes
                that have no flag and no word for *parade*
                my spine
                        knows
                                African drums
                                        in night-fire
                                                air

joyous jousting of jiving joints dives so deeply
hinges of the day   let loose
doors locked shut now flap
in breezes of dance

problems&plans desires&pains
        melt
in cauldron of music and movement

set free   through sweat

after trunk and limbs plant and cultivate
after music rests   after I exit
the mirrored studio   skin damp-drying
as I eat or read or stroll down the street
every organ and bone
        still hums and shimmies   everybody happy

Tantrum

A rare night of husband out,
home to myself, a gift
of my own noise or silence, but
the calendar holds the graduation invitation
of a friend's valedictorian daughter. I celebrate
this milestone, wish my joy for them to be my gift to them,
but hours across town with them
will carve my evening,

home sliced to a sliver.
Impossible, both evenings I want in one.
The choices launch torpedoes at each other:
too selfish, too indulgent, too lonely,
too unfriendly, not nurturing,
not restful, not cozy, not fun.
Too much chatter.
Each choice gutted.
I sink. *I want*
too much. I am
not

enough.
The wounded girl within
rises like a ghost
in this push and pull of self or other.
I turn to this exasperated child I've become, *tell me*
what you want, what will please you.
In rare spotlight, she unveils an urge,
knife-edged and sticky,

to slip away as before,
to numb out, bliss out
on sugar and bloat, block out

all the *too much* and *not enough*. She
throws a tantrum for the one thing
my care will allow no longer.
Her demands bruise me
but cannot crack
the encircling wall

of my love.
She unclenches her fist from
what she can no longer have, nibbles
what she has always really wanted—
not yet sure of the taste.

Husband's Breath

On my shoulder at night, his breath
    whispers, tickles, promises,
        pools under my flesh.

His breath is the blanket
    snuggled by a toddler,
        eyes of a grandparent

upon the newborn,
    ice melt in spring.
        His breath seeps through the sieve of my skin,

quenches the outstretched tongue
    of my twirling, mirthful girl,
        dandelion releasing

her seeds into his breeze,
    beginnings hidden,
        tight as a fist until

his sweet sigh ushers the girl
    into this home only
        only only

for who she is,
    holy holy
        wholly the self who once couldn't be.

Now I can inhale,
    bathe, soak, splash
        since I broke trail,

deciphering the girl's cries,
  once trapped, echoing
    off the walls of wounds,

gate open only to need,
  closed to receive
    his breath, here in my palm,

my own trade winds, all along.

Mirror

once when he and I made love on the king-size bed
    in the wall of mirrors
on the sliding closet doors of the Brown Palace Hotel,
    she was there

more often in a glimpse after showering, before dressing,
free of lines and colors of clothing to cut or distract from curves,
    moments come
when the mirror reflects
    the me my husband sees
like the aha! figure emerging from an optical illusion

these images sanctify breasts, belly, thighs, hips
    evaluations of *too much* and *not right*
        slide away and slither out of sight
            comparison grows mute
    the word *flaw* redefines itself
        into *unique, estimable*
            as with silk, leather, marble
                only the words *care* and *yes* make sense

years of his compliments no longer dismissed
as mere kindness—they're suddenly simply self evident
    and celebratory

ah, yes, there I am
        pumpkins and plums
        pears and peppers
        oranges and almonds

teacups of breasts
white moon of belly
    let abdomen exhale fully
      inhale roundly
all the soft sexy supple succulence
the world could love
    woman as she is

I head into my day, and I hope she remains
    in the mirror at just that angle in just that light
presenting her luminous self not for my husband's perusal
      but for my extended embrace

Hiking a Trail of Turns

He approaches from a distance, no other
hiker seen all morning. T-shirt sleeveless
and shorts short, he looks

imported—Italian—I imagine.
We exchange smiles as we pass. Solid biceps,
broad shoulders, curved quadriceps elicit

between my legs, a faint stir just short
of a purr and—an urge to bolt,
an inkling of how those muscled arms

could harm. Even before
the trail turns down through berry bushes
by the stream, breezes carry away

the shed fur of fear,
this old, foreboding companion
who used to whittle desire into a blade of shame,

who slapped whispers into silence. What fills me
here is the hum of golden grass
orchestrated by morning sun heating

these foothills, older than any sin.
What frolics with me is the sweet scent
rising from today's meadow at mid-life.

What surprises is this delight peeking out,
harmless sprig of sprightly lust
warm as the air on my bared arms

this ripe August. Past decades elapsed blank
and chilled through breasts and pelvis—numbness
broad as a mare's back, skittish to contact,

only silver screen crushes and masturbation
fantasies, until my husband's touch tended
unmuscled desires and remained day after day,

horse whisperer to my hesitation.
Groomed by the hands of our marriage
of a decade and a half, trust must be

ranging farther afield late in the season.
Relief and resilience lope through grasses
blowing on both sides of this trail of turns

where the unexpected and exquisite
arrive in small, subtle twists,
brilliant and brief as wildflowers.

Gap, Bridge

An arm stretches halfway across
the years unspoken, extends
to offer contact, discovers
thin air of doubt
                    where trust could
bolster it, but only lonely
                              ambivalence echoes.

Firm on earth,
like a crane swinging the arm into place,
rests a heart that once found safety
only with the sturdy fence of distance
and now knows
enclosure constricts
and now knows the next step toward fullness includes

his wounds that became
my wounds, includes
setting down a plank
in the midst of the fog of my fear.

Fingers unfurl,
willing to risk encounter
with my father bound still in his ball
                    of narcissism
                                   and need
I fear this bridge won't bear.

My arm hovers as if hundreds
of gemstone-hued hummingbirds
flutter to hold it.

Awaiting his reply
(and then curious about my own response),
I watch residue
cascade off fingertips,
tears of the girl I still contain
                                    but no longer am,
wailing for the father he never
can be. Pain shines
like rain under the rays of a sun
stretching toward embrace.

Breakfast at Fratelli's

My father reaches eighty the month we meet
after six-and-a-half years of estrangement.
I enter the cafe where my mouth of dust
transforms into an impulsive kiss when I see
trifocals, gray plaid shirt, a wooden cane
against the bench—and him, frail, shaky, soft.
I sit and he speaks of recent travels and health
maladies and a mechanic who tried to rip him off
and the success of his career ended sixteen years
prior. He insists on paying, *My treat.* I listen,
the wooden bench hard beneath me. The ceiling fan
throws shadows around, incessant and familiar.

Family Geography

Notes jingle—soft and cheery,
technological, my nephew's soundtrack,
a little icing for my ear.
Visiting boy on couch slumps,
neck bent deeply forward, only
sleek black hair, fingers and buttons, eyes
and screen. Game Boy cartoon cars
race before, race between, race behind
movie, museum, Monopoly. His car always wins
the checkered flag, I see,
over his shoulder.

His great grandparents, my grandparents, left
Poland, left family, settled
among other immigrants, pasts unspoken
in the hills and tunnels of a Pennsylvania coal town.

My parents left poverty, left family, settled
in the Rocky Mountain West among other income
seekers, far from who they were
before shiny 1950s suburbia.

I see my mother to her death.
From the East, not one relative.

I see my father's shaking fist.
Six figures barely dent his poverty.

I see my brother and sister scatter
farther west, huddle against the next ocean, blend
into professions among other physicians, programmers.

The woman who will become my brother's wife
leaves her land of birth, all
her relatives, to live a Mercedes
life in sparkling Silicon Valley.

Nine months after
the wedding, their son is born.

Lacking sibling and cousin, he is oceans away
from most who would adore him.

He is the pool at the bottom
of his families' waterfall, this strange
lineage of estrangement,
this sea of silence.

He silences Game Boy to tell me
how he came to love airplanes
when I ask.

Technology sits sidelined and hushed
while we play Huggermugger, our favorite
board game. I simplify the questions
less each summer while we nibble his chosen
cookies, giggle over his school
stories. We spin the spinner until the wished-for
number receives its aim, coax each other's
list of rhymes, ignore the plastic hourglass,
pretend time doesn't run out.

Together we haunt county airports, runway air
full of jet fuel, engine roar, and blasts of wind, dominated
by machines made sleek and powerful by technology
and men proficient in their work. Prepubescent eyes
seek planes he longs to pilot, to fly away

someday. I reach
to weave a small nest of family
so his flights will not release
him from us into air but propel
him into his own whole future, fully rooted.

Pocketing the Stones

Again at the monastery, breakfasts
are held in the privilege of silence.
Every morning I lift an orange
or pear from the wooden sideboard.
I slice through it with the communal
knife. I carry it to the garden,
even if the chill brings shivers.
Seated under porch or pine, I savor
every bit, count each bite
as is the practice here
of mindful eating.

She returns to me—as if
we have never met,
the innocence I was before
the binges:

        young girl who sits on the wall
        silent wall of stone

        young girl eats a peach sucks its juice
        guides her teeth around the pit
        stone that lies at the center

        blond hair glistens in the sun
        morning dew dandelion seed

        sharp edges crack
        old wall stands softly
        air and light flow the past let go
        where once solid stone

breezes blow wisps of her hair
onto the peach juiciness of her face
she swings her legs ankles crossed
she wanted to wear
her cheery checkered yellow dress
Nana made her wear
corduroy jeans and darned sweater
belly and arms safe from chill
warm under wool in the sun
bottom and legs safe from cold
stone and edges
that could shave
skin draw blood

the girl finishes the flesh of the fruit
holds in her sticky palm the remnant pit
future fruit heavy as a pebble
she tosses it away

long standing wall is becoming home
small life burrows in crevices to safety
along edges stray seeds find pockets
dormant nourishment
stories wait
for a voice to come

the girl will birth her self upon the wall
attachment to what has come before
all she will never know
she will want no need of it
though it has need of her
thick as blood

she puts a stone one heavy stone
into each of her two pockets
she begins to walk
upon the wall crumbling footing
weighted but balanced
upon the wall she teaches herself
to skip

her small body warms the stone
small voice sings darkness in daylight
the wall comes alive
like a snake in the sun

Maybe the wall never was
what it seemed.

Arrive

Outside the shrine, mountain breezes
run through my hair like horses
through windswept fields.

In the stupa, the golden Buddha waits,
androgynous and twenty feet tall. Long
fingers curve. Craving could
curl up in those hands,
quietly weep itself to sleep.

One hundred and three books
of ancient teachings reside
inside the cushion upon which the statue rests.
The chest encloses the skull of a teacher revered.
Filling every hollow of the body, prayers

painted by monks,
saffron ink
on rice paper,
rolled and wrapped
in yellow ribbons,
twenty-two million,
two hundred forty-nine thousand,
three hundred times.

Peace seeping in,
my every breath
becomes a breeze
redolent of belonging.

Rearranging the Landscape

Into the bare light of daybreak,
wings flutter, my foot lifts, headlight smacks

the fledgling. Air-filled bones snap,
the body hurled aside, tossed like trash.

Is the bird stunned? suffering? already dead? I don't
stop, a pickup fills the rearview, inertia presses my pedal.

I cup pain in my hands as I would nestle
this broken-winged bird   or a betrayed child.

I vow that this once I will not jettison myself
to suffering   or substances.

My crushed lungs fill with warm breath.
My shoulders draw back, wings about to take flight.

Baptized in the dawn of forgiveness
for a life I have bloodied and abandoned,

I wish the same mercy
for my father.

Behold

I am the poet daughter
of a man who knows machines—
his weekends spent measuring spark plug gaps
on our Ford and Chevy, weekdays calculating
trajectories of Viking spacecrafts to Mars.

Though willing to fiddle with or fix
the washer, the dollhouse, the bike,
he is barely held to us, his family.
All he can toss at us are highflying
expositions about his work.
Passageways are what he sees, far
above the heads of earthbound humans.

Science, engineering, and exploration
remain his line, stanza, and verse.
The poet daughter practices telemetry
with rhythm and rhyme, evaluates the payload
of images, plans the touchdown of metaphors
—to him, little aliens.

Exploration leaves her willing to release her loyalty
to the egocentric view, to edit the old stories
with curious eyes within the constellations
of entire lives, like Galileo searching
for what was once unseen, finding that everything
does not circle her.

The poet daughter polishes the lenses
of her words, the telescope through which she perceives
their link, father and daughter,
her devotion strung to photographs from Hubble
revealing splendors never before imagined.

Under the Words

This one is made of bone china, he says. The slender,
ten-inch tall Emperor Penguin is lifted
from the shelf by fingers too weak to peel
open half-and-half containers for coffee.
My father's trembling hands cradle it for my view.

Nine approaches on the mantel clock
in his senior living condominium
made into a cozy nest for two
by the woman he married
within the year of my mother's death.
Rain gathers with darkness on streets below.

*This one is hand-blown glass. I met the artist
when I bought it for Dee at Christmas.* The glassmith
bestowed the cartoonish skating penguin
with a sleek wingspan and a frozen body of joy.

We may be halfway through his wife's collection,
though my father chooses randomly
off the nine shelves of this lit hutch filled
with nothing but penguins.

This was a gift from her granddaughter.
The lead-glass crystal holds the weight of years.

*One of the neighbors found this in the gutter,
cleaned it up and gave it to us.* He chuckles
over a chunky wooden penguin, a child's
toy, most of the paint chipped off.

This one is from Russia. The painted penguin parent
pokes its beak toward a chick peeking up
from its perch on the parent's feet
where it would rest protected
through Antarctic winter storms
within paternal layers of fat and feathers.

By the door waits my red umbrella, held
afloat earlier in my steady hand,
our vinyl alcove sheltering us through his small steps
into Joy Luck Restaurant where he ensured
the hostess and waiter and bus boy knew
I was his daughter.

Now water gains force against the windows.
Where's this little guy from, Dad? I point to a burst
of blue the size of my thumbnail.

Despite his age spots, severe hunch,
dependence on a walker...
despite my years of hours seeking
counsel, sitting in meditation, dissecting
books on assertiveness...

remarkably little has changed in our exchanges.

Except for one thing: Under the words, I hear
he is saying what I need to know.

I don't care about the penguins.
I don't care that my day began hours before dawn
and that on the tired drive home, spotty wipers and wet
reflections will tax my weak night vision.
I care that he may crave company
while his wife is out of town.
No wounds are left to protect.

The tight fist has opened
to let the past wash away.

Ocean of Recovery

An island is what I wanted. I believed
if I swam long and hard, if I followed
broken-lined treasure maps of therapists,

if I tinkered with my internal compass,
I would one day climb up onto the rocks of
The Island, deep water behind, boundary clear

—even if wavering and wave-swept—sure footing
of *this*, *not that*, *now* distinct from *then*,
a wide beach between *eating disorder* and *recovery*.

I am still swimming.
This ocean breathes, rises and falls.
I breathe, chest rising and falling.

Is it the disorder sighting others seemingly secure
on sun-drenched South Pacific green peaks,
solid above my daily uncertain sea?

No thatched roof here. Storms churn. Doldrums pass.
Beacons to mark passage or guide onward are scarce,
lost in the chop. Undercurrents yank. Tides surge.

Is it the disorder that seeks The Island, thinks
only wet or dry, chants *tomorrow* and *someday*,
plants doubts that I might be dog paddling in circles?

Dark shapes still attack out of the depths,
but I glide from the grasp of sharp teeth once
inescapable. Recovery trickles through cupped palms.

I navigate with others swimming in recovery.
We rest like a raft of pelicans, buoying each other,
floating, having learned enough to trust.

Vaster than any island, the ocean of possibility
breathes me. This recovery that gave me my life
rises and falls. We are one.

Frog Song

In places wilder than home, creaks and groans
of frog song come to me: dusk to dawn
musicals in a monastery garden, fragments
through New Zealand rain, today

from the mountain marsh
down the path below the window
where I write, stepping stones back
into memory and forward into faith,

bridging the splinters of ache and trust.
Some amphibian vestige at the base of my spine
throbs along to their rhythm. Alone for days,
my pen and I let frogs dictate

poems. Uninvited, loneliness
crashes the party, cloaking herself
in her usual costume, a shove
toward kitchen cupboards. Not running

from the discomfort into the arms of food,
I listen to the song of my own
longing. I take loneliness
for a stroll. I hold her

shriveled hand. I kiss her damp forehead.
She clenches my heart. I am with her
and she is with me, twins now complete,
neither of us abandoned.

Cool evening, damp trail, soft ground
cushion the fall of pain unclasping.
I could be a frog here, belly damp, sweet earth
just under my nose. The chorus of my kind

would be my stepping stones, notes in air.
I'm not scared here, loneliness confesses.
Neither am I, I say. I tuck her into
the chambers of my throbbing heart.

Moving On: One to Another

Ptarmigan cluck softly, one to another,
to keep with each other.
Otherwise dissolving into stone,
their voices unveil them,

connect them to their bodies. On Quandary Peak,
I summon my body to elevate me above
fourteen-thousand feet. Not alone—
Susan before, Terry behind.

Up and up each step a ladder rung
hung up a wall up above trees
up to nothing but rocks and a drop
of nothing but space

sheer and slippery as fear.
Above is wind and above is mist.
Sharp edges echo silence
and hold me.

Legs ache. Lungs suck dry air.
Just like vanishing into freshman year
just like merging into corporate America
just like turning the knob into therapy

like the masks cracked, one by one,
and, with them, others' dreams, I wonder,
how does anyone do this?
Still, we go up—until I look down

the rocks of return, down the corner of the peak,
how high the climb, what's been left behind,
down the stern plunge to journey's flat start.
Panic yanks the last air from hungry lungs.

Terry enfolds me,
instructs each breath.
Susan shelters me,
begins to sing,

you are my sunshine. Breath
returns. My breath. And feet,
steps, mine, but none mine alone.
Lifted by air, I rise now as a prayer

flag, stitched by pain,
flapping against gusts of all the old voices,
connected to the flesh of ground
found by taking the trail of the next step.

One line binds like hands held—
everybody bears scars.
Victim of nothing and no one, I no longer
see tragedy here—only life.

ACKNOWLEDGMENTS

This book has been lived and written over years, and there are many I wish to thank who helped me to speak my hunger or who helped to create *Hunger Speaks*:

the staff at Porter's Eating Disorder Clinic,
    Joan Shapiro, M.D., and Cindy Brody, LCSW;

the Monday evening circle of journal writers led by
    Kathleen Adams,
the monthly writers' coaching group led by
    Cynthia Morris,
the Friday morning circle of creative writers led by
    Deb McLeod, and
the fine poets of Lighthouse Writers master class led by
    Denver Poet Laureate Chris Ransick;

readers Mike Henry, Karen Lehmann, Kathleen Adams,
    Susan Coppage Evans, and Joy Sawyer;

fellow writers, friends, and fans of *Hunger Speaks*:
    Fran Becker, Aevea Finkelman, Fran Jenner,
    Ani Liggett, Karen Sbrockey, Tama Kieves,
    Dana Bennett, Eleanor Keefer, Kimberly McClintock,
    and Rosanne Sterne;

providers of various forms of sustenance:
    Sandra Garcia, Lucinda Williams, Steve Balcerovich,
    and the Benedictine sisters at Benet Pines Retreat
    Center: Josie, Olive, and Phyllis;

and creative partners who transformed my collection of poems into a book:

> Dr. Patricia Ross of Roberts & Ross, Sheila Hentges, and Faye Quam Heimerl.

Immeasurable thanks to my husband Terry (provider of exemplary systems administrative support) who made this book possible because he never wavered in his belief in my writing or in me.

Without each of these people generously providing a necessary stepping stone, *Hunger Speaks* would have remained a hazy dream rather than become a solid book.

ABOUT THE AUTHOR

Carolyn Jennings gratefully celebrates more than twenty years of side-by-side recovery and writing. She has built a practice of expressing what would otherwise be blurred into silence. She resides in Colorado with her sweet husband, trunks of filled journals, and one bright shelf of books with blank pages.

Carolyn's focus and joy have expanded beyond her own personal writing; she now offers workshops presenting the journal techniques that add wings to her life.

You can reach Carolyn via **www.writingourwings.com**.

CPSIA information can be obtained
at www.ICGtesting.com
Printed in the USA
LVHW09s0325101018
593080LV00001B/205/P